MW01247992

Amazon founder Jeff Bezos

AMAZON

ODYSSEYS

SARA GILBERT

CREATIVE EDUCATION · CREATIVE PAPERBACKS

Published by Creative Education and Creative Paperbacks
P.O. Box 227, Mankato, Minnesota 56002
Creative Education and Creative Paperbacks
are imprints of The Creative Company
www.thecreativecompany.us

Design by Graham Morgan
Art direction by Tom Morgan
Edited by Jill Kalz

Images by Alamy (Kristoffer Tripplaar, Jack Young, WorldFoto),
Getty (Joe Raedle, Johnny Milano/Bloomberg, Joshua Lott/
Bloomberg, Justin Sullivan, Ken James/Bloomberg, Kevin
Schafer, Michael Kovac, Paul Hawthorne, Ryder/Bloomberg.
Spencer Platt, Thinkstock), Pexels (Anna Shvets, Erik
Mclean, Stephanie Ho, ThisIsEngineering), Unsplash
(Alexandra Tran, Andrew Stickelman, ANIRUDH, Anshu A,
Christian Wiediger, engin akyurt, Kaitlyn Baker, rupixen.
com, Vivint Solar), Wikimedia Commons (Acroterion,
Bonnachoven, Mathieu Thouvenin, Michael Fleischhacker)

Copyright © 2025 Creative Education, Creative Paperbacks
International copyright reserved in all countries.
No part of this book may be reproduced in any form
without written permission from the publisher.

Library of Congress Cataloging-in-Publication Data
Names: Gilbert, Sara, author.
Title: Amazon / by Sara Gilbert.
Description: Mankato, Minnesota : Creative Education and
    Creative Paperbacks, 2025. | Series: Odysseys in business |
    Includes bibliographical references and index. | Audience:
    Ages 12–15 | Audience: Grades 7–9 | Summary: "A business
    survey for young adults of the online shopping giant Amazon,
    covering the Web-based global retail company's technology
    and services, history, and founder, Jeff Bezos. Includes
    sidebars, a glossary, and further resources"—Provided by
    publisher.
Identifiers: LCCN 2023046552 (print) | LCCN 2023046553
    (ebook) | ISBN 9781640269149 (library binding) | ISBN
    9781682774649 (paperback) | ISBN 9798889890829
    (ebook)
Subjects: LCSH: Amazon.com (Firm)—Juvenile literature. |
    Electronic commerce—Juvenile literature.
Classification: LCC HF5548.32 .G525 2025 (print) | LCC
    HF5548.32 (ebook) DDC 381/.142065—dc23/eng/20231207
LC record available at https://lccn.loc.gov/2023046552
LC ebook record available at https://lccn.loc.gov/2023046553

Printed in China

streaming
movies & tv

prime

fast & free

CONTENTS

Introduction

Shortly after the Amazon.com website launched on July 16, 1995, a loud beep echoed through the company's offices near downtown Seattle, Washington. The beep alerted the Amazon.com staff that a customer had made a purchase. The beep sounded six more times that day and was accompanied each time by a cheer from Amazon employees.

OPPOSITE: The iconic observation tower called the Space Needle overlooks downtown Seattle, a city of more than 750,000 people.

But those beeps quickly became more frequent—and more distracting to the small staff. In its first week, the company logged more than $12,000 worth of purchases.

Within a couple weeks, the bell had become so distracting that it had to be disabled. And it would be almost impossible to keep up with sales today. In 2021, the company sold more than 13.5 billion individual items. At least 19 orders are placed on Amazon.com every second. Almost 66,000 products are shipped out from one

In its early days, Amazon shipped most items in heavy corrugated cardboard boxes.

OPPOSITE The Amazon River carries more fresh water into the oceans than any other river in the world.

of the company's more than 200 fulfillment centers around the world every hour.

Like its namesake—the Amazon River in South America—Amazon.com is famous for being the largest. Company founder Jeff Bezos referenced the river on November 1, 1994, the day he registered the URL for his new online bookstore. "This is not only the largest river in the world," he said, "it's many times larger than the next biggest river. It blows all other rivers away."

AMAZON

By the Book

Drive west. This was the only instruction that Jeff Bezos and his wife, MacKenzie, gave the movers who had packed up their Manhattan apartment in the summer of 1994. Bezos promised to call them with a specific destination the next day. At the age of 30, Bezos had just quit his job as a rising star at a New York investment company. He had a vision for an online bookstore.

OPPOSITE: Jeff Bezos transformed the book-buying experience, turning physical shopping carts into virtual ones.

Bezos knew that he needed to build his headquarters in a city that embraced technology, was flush with recent college graduates, and was near a large book distribution center. So, he called the movers and told them to head for Seattle, Washington. Seattle was the home of software company Microsoft and the University of Washington. It was also just a six-hour drive from Ingram Book Group, one of the largest book distributors in the country.

With MacKenzie driving a 1988 Chevy Blazer they had borrowed from his dad, Bezos rode shotgun and filled spreadsheets with revenue projections for his Internet-based business. He was excited about the World Wide Web, which had only begun to be used by the public in the fall of 1993. He could see the potential for online commerce and knew that he had to build his business before every other entrepreneur also figured that out. He chose books as his business. He knew that they were easy to purchase from publishers and distributors. He knew that books were affordable and that people liked to buy them. And Bezos was confident that building his bookstore on the Web, without the overhead of a brick-and-mortar store, would allow him to offer better deals than traditional booksellers could.

When they got to Seattle, Bezos and MacKenzie rented a small home with an attached one-car garage. That garage became the company's first office in November 1994. Bezos had recruited two programmers—Sheldon Kaphan and Paul Davis—to work with him. He made desks for all three of them out of plain wooden doors from Home Depot. Then they got busy figuring out the website's technical details, including what it

AMAZON

would look like and how it would store information about customers' orders. Bezos, Kaphan, and Davis relied on open-source software to develop the framework for the online bookstore. Open-source software is a set of programs programmers write and then make available to other programmers at no charge.

At the same time, Bezos was trying to secure financial backing for the company. His family had invested almost $250,000 in exchange for stock in the business, which was incorporated as Amazon.com in

Technology drives every part of Amazon's business.

Garage Power

Jeff Bezos had only one requirement when he and his wife were looking for a house to rent in Seattle: It had to have a garage. Many of the entrepreneurs whom Bezos admired had started in their garages—including Steve Jobs, who created Apple with his friend Steve Wozniak in his parents' garage. Perhaps it was a sign of things to come when Amazon's computers and other equipment maxed out the space's electrical capacity in a matter of months. Bezos joked that electricity was the reason companies had to move out of garages. "It's not that they run out of room," he said. "It's that they run out of electrical power."

February 1995. That was enough money to hire a few employees and to move into a larger space in Seattle's industrial district just in time for the website's official launch on July 16, 1995.

Sales trickled in until Yahoo!, a Web search engine, placed Amazon.com on its "What's Cool" list three days after launch. Traffic on the site increased rapidly. At the end of the first week, Amazon.com had tallied $12,438 in orders. At that pace, the company expected revenues of $5 million in its first year. But it needed additional money up front to hire more employees, upgrade equipment, and develop its services.

Bezos was willing to wait for his company to make money—his original business plan had predicted that it would be five years before the company would turn a **profit**. But Amazon.com needed funds to remain in business. With the help of friends, Bezos secured $981,000 in private funding by the end of 1995. And then, thanks to a glowing article about Amazon in the *Wall Street Journal* on May 16, 1996, more investors

Bezos could see the potential for online commerce and knew that he had to build his Web-based business before every other entrepreneur also figured that out.

started calling. Kleiner Perkins Caufield & Byers, a venture capital firm that invested in new tech startups, provided $8 million in exchange for a 13 percent stake in the company.

Bezos was able to hire more managers, warehouse workers, and customer service agents. With the number of employees growing, however, the company had to move into a larger office building in downtown Seattle. It also had to purchase a 93,000-square-foot (8,640-square-meter) warehouse facility. The company's staggering

growth led to another move as well: selling shares of Amazon on the stock market. On May 15, 1997, the day of its initial public offering, Amazon raised $54 million. Bezos and his family members—including his mom, dad, brother, and sister—immediately became millionaires. So did many of the employees who had been promised stock as part of their payment package.

By October 1997, just two years after Amazon had launched, the one-millionth customer placed an order. Bezos flew to Japan to personally deliver

Rufus at Work

When Jeff Bezos hired Eric and Susan Benson to work at
Amazon early in its history, he got a third "employee" as well.
Every day, the couple brought their pet corgi, Rufus, to the office
with them. Rufus became an unofficial mascot for Amazon.
Bezos even asked the landlord of one of the company's early
buildings to write the dog into the lease. Before any new feature
of the website was launched, Rufus had to tap his paw on the
keyboard. Although Rufus is now long gone, thousands of other

the two books—a computer text and a biography of Princess Diana—to the customer. At the end of the year, Amazon had made $147.8 million, an 838 percent jump over the previous year. But because it was adding employees, investing in new buildings, and increasing its marketing budget, the company again lost more money than it made.

Bezos was under pressure to show a profit. Instead of tightening his belt, however, he made several acquisitions. He positioned Amazon as a one-stop shopping site, not just a bookseller. By 1999, Amazon's eight million customers could buy books, music, and DVDs, as well as electronics, toys and games, home improvement products, software, video games, and gifts. The company had 5,000 employees and multiple locations—including sites in Germany and the United Kingdom. But it was still losing money.

That didn't deter the editors of *Time* magazine from naming Bezos the Person of the Year for 1999. Amid rapid growth in online businesses, the magazine described the 35-year-old Internet entrepreneur as "unquestionably, the king of cybercommerce." It lauded his efforts to help "build the foundation of our future."

With a credit card and a few clicks on a computer, consumers can buy almost anything on Amazon.

Pushing for Profits

The unchecked optimism surrounding Web-based businesses between 1995 and 2000 led to widespread adoption of the Internet as part of daily life, for both business and pleasure. Shoppers were becoming more comfortable spending money online, and investors were eager to put large amounts of money into new start-up companies built on websites.

OPPOSITE: In 2005, under the leadership of Jeff Bezos, Amazon celebrated its 10th year on a high note.

Those investments and high expectations for profitability caused the stock market to skyrocket. But in the spring of 2000, just as Bezos was planning for Amazon.com to show its first profit, the financial bubble building around the surge in dot-com companies burst. Many of the start-ups that had received hopeful funding from investors hadn't able to turn a profit. Around the same time, interest rates started going up, which made it harder to borrow money. In reaction, the stock market index plunged by more than 700 percent in a matter of weeks. Dozens of new dot-com companies disappeared almost immediately. Others struggled to stay afloat.

Amazon.com was in a better position than most, but it didn't escape the bust unharmed. The value of its stock took a steep drop, and shareholders were angry.

The media, which had praised Bezos for his clever ideas just a few months earlier, turned critical. The company was labeled with such nicknames as "Amazon.bomb" and "Amazon.toast" as critics predicted the company's collapse. "You go from Internet poster child to Internet whipping boy," Bezos said in a *Fortune* magazine article in December 2000. "It takes, like, 30 seconds."

The pressure to show a profit ramped up. As 2000 ended, Bezos sent an email to all Amazon employees announcing the company's internal goal to turn a profit

Fulfillment center employees receive goods, pick and pack orders, and ship those orders to customers.

within the next year. "We're aiming to have sales of $5 billion, produce over $1 billion in gross profits, and achieve solid operating profitability," he wrote.

Of course, to make that happen, Bezos had to make deep cuts to Amazon's operations. He laid off 1,300 workers, closed 2 warehouses and a customer-service center, and brought in experts to help streamline the business's processes. He also purged products that weren't profitable from the site's offerings. Then, he forged a partnership with bookstore giant Borders to foster cooperation, rather than competition, between the two businesses.

But the company continued to struggle. Bezos's goal went unrealized. Amazon reported a staggering net loss of $567 million in 2001 and of $149 million in 2002. In each year, a strong holiday season had led to fourth-quarter profits, which were encouraging. And although it was still limping along financially, Amazon was now being called a survivor. Many online retailers, including Boo.com and Pets.com, had shut down completely. Amazon was one of the few e-commerce companies still in business after the devastating dot-com bust.

Amazon's progress toward profitability continued in 2003. Customers responded positively to newly implemented price cuts and the addition of clothing and accessories to Amazon's inventory. They were also drawn to the offer of free shipping on certain orders over $25. But it was a book that helped propel the company to its first profitable year: *Harry Potter and the Order of the Phoenix,* the fifth book in the popular Harry Potter series by author J. K. Rowling. Customers were able to place advance orders for the book starting on January 15. By the time it was officially released on June 21, more than 1.3 million copies had been pre-ordered worldwide—more than any other product that had been available during Amazon's eight-year history.

Those sales, combined with a fantastic holiday season and growth in international sales—Amazon had sites in six countries, including Canada, Japan, and France—the company reported a profit of $35 million in 2003. Having met that critical benchmark, Amazon suddenly seemed to be able to make money easily. On a single day during the 2004 holiday season, customers ordered more than 2.8 million items from

Amazon Reviews

One of the earliest features added to Amazon.com was the ability to add reviews, which Shel Kaphan coded over a weekend in June 1995. Although Kaphan and other Amazon employees wrote the first book reviews, it didn't take long for others to join in—or to add a bit of humor. Shoppers have left creative reviews for everything from Bic pens to gummi bears. One long, descriptive review of sugar-free gummi bears ended with this line:

"Not only did they cause me to fail my final test, but the anguish I experienced is something I wouldn't wish upon anyone, not even my worst enemy."

the website. That day helped push total sales for the year up to $6.9 billion.

Bezos was in a celebratory mood for Amazon's 10th birthday in 2005. In addition to hosting a party that featured famed musicians Bob Dylan and Norah Jones, the company introduced Amazon Prime. This new program provided free two-day and discounted shipping for an annual fee of $79. Although Prime became quite popular with customers, its rollout was worrisome to many inside the company and to Wall Street analysts. They saw it eating away at overall revenues. During the first three months of 2005, for example, Amazon spent $167 million on shipping costs. Only a fraction of that was paid back by customers. Add to that the cost of hiring computer programmers to perfect Amazon's search engine and further tweak the site's features. There was also a growing marketing budget, which was dedicated almost

"If we take care of customers, the stock will take care of itself in the long term."

entirely to email campaigns and promotions. Bezos considered all of those initiatives part of his plan to put customers first, instead of focusing on profits. "If we take care of customers, the stock will take care of itself in the long term," he said.

To prove his point, Bezos spent most of 2006 expanding the services, products, and features available through Amazon.com. In November, the company was voted number one in customer service in a National Retail Survey. December sales eclipsed all previous holiday sales records, thanks in large part to products such as Apple iPods and Nintendo Wii gaming systems. Even so, the company's profits of $190 million were considered a disappointment.

Beyond Books

Despite disappointing revenues, Bezos had a reason to be optimistic about his company's future in 2007. For three years, Amazon's developers had been secretly working on what they called "Project A": a portable electronic reader that would be able to **download** digital content such as books, articles, and more.

OPPOSITE: Started in 2017, Amazon Air (originally Amazon Prime Air) transports goods between the company's distribution centers.

Fedorovna. With these words she greeted Prince Vasili Kuragin, a man of high rank and importance, who was the first to arrive at her reception. Anna Pavlovna had had a cough for some days. She was, as she said, suffering from la grippe; grippe being then a new word in St. Petersburg, used only by the elite.

All her invitations without exception, written in French, and delivered by a scarlet-liveried footman that morning, ran as follows:

"If you have nothing better to do, Count (or Prince), and if the prospect of spending an evening with a poor invalid is not too terrible, I shall be very charmed to see you tonight between 7 and 10—Annette Scherer."

"Heavens! what a virulent attack!" replied the prince, not in the least disconcerted by this reception. He had just entered, wearing an embroidered court uniform, knee breeches, and shoes, and had stars on his breast and a

Press ⊙ to show number of highlighters

By 2010, the Kindle device was Amazon's most gifted product.

"The baby boomers have a love affair with paper. But the next-gen people, in their 20s and below, do everything on a screen."

Similar products made by companies such as Sony were already in the market, but Amazon believed its product would provide a better experience for readers. On November 19, 2007, Amazon released the Kindle—its first self-made product. It immediately started selling more than 90,000 digital books, including almost all the current *New York Times* bestsellers and new releases, at a flat rate of $9.99.

One of the Kindle's main distinctions from earlier e-readers was its ability to download books without connecting to a computer. That high-tech convenience, combined with its compact size and easy-to-read lighted screen, was especially appealing to a younger audience. "The baby boomers have a love affair with paper," said novelist James Patterson when the Kindle was launched. "But the next-gen people, in their 20s and below, do everything on a screen."

All 250,000 of the $399 Kindles in Amazon's original inventory sold out within hours of the launch. The replacement batch disappeared just as quickly when popular talk show host Oprah Winfrey had Bezos on her show. Digital books accounted for 10 percent of Amazon's total book sales for the year, even though only 200,000 titles, just a fraction of the millions of books available on Amazon, were ready for download. Readers had clearly embraced the Kindle technology. "This is

Amazon Down

It can be frustrating when a website has technical difficulties. For an e-commerce site such as Amazon.com, it can also be quite costly. Consider what happened in August 2013, when the site stopped working for almost 40 minutes. Shoppers saw this message: "Oops! We're very sorry, but we're having trouble doing what you just asked us to do. Please give us another chance—click the Back button on your browser and try your request again." By the time service was restored, the company had lost almost $5 million in sales, considering that in the previous quarter they had recorded $15.7 billion in sales, which equals about $120,000 every minute.

the most important thing we've ever done," Bezos said. "It's so ambitious to take something as highly evolved as the book and improve on it—and maybe even change the way people read."

Amazon released an upgraded version of the Kindle in 2009 to keep up with new e-readers released by Barnes & Noble and Sony. By that time, almost 400,000 digital books were available on the website. Amazon had purchased audiobook company Audible in 2008, gaining access to its immense library of digital materials. For

Amazon's smartphone, called Fire Phone, was not a hit with consumers.

the first time in company history, e-books sold better than printed books during the holiday shopping season.

Even as developers continued working on upgrades to the Kindle, "Project B" was already in the works: a smartphone. Work on the project began in 2010, just

"It's so ambitious to take something as highly evolved as the book and improve on it—and maybe even change the way people read."

as Apple was releasing the iPhone 4. Despite efforts to keep it under wraps, media speculation was rampant in the years leading up to the Fire Phone's release in July 2014. One of the stories reported that the phone would be offered for free to Amazon Prime members. In fact, the phones cost $199 for the 32GB version and $299 for the 64GB version. Some of the earliest buyers were rewarded for their purchase with a free Prime membership.

Unlike the Kindle, however, Amazon's Fire Phone didn't lure customers away from the existing smartphone options. Its most unique attribute was "Dynamic Perspective," which used four front-facing cameras and a gyroscope to track the user's eyes and give the screen an almost 3D sense of depth. Even that feature didn't create enough buzz around the phone. By August 2015, the Fire Phone was no longer available on Amazon.com.

By then, however, Amazon's attention had shifted to "Project D," its third successful hardware launch (Project C was abandoned before coming to market). In November 2014, the company released the Amazon Echo, a smart speaker that was powered by Alexa, the artificial intelligence "voice" of the product. Although it was first available only to Amazon Prime members, by the 2015 holiday season, the Echo device was available in more than 3,000 retail stores throughout the United States. That year, more than one million Echoes were

Making News

In August 2013, Jeff Bezos offered to pay $250 million of his own money to purchase *The Washington Post*, a newspaper published in Washington, D.C., that was struggling financially. Bezos decided to make the newspaper a private company instead of a publicly traded one. As such, he didn't have to report earnings to shareholders. Although Bezos was too busy running Amazon to get involved in the day-to-day operations of *The Washington Post*, some assumed that he was using it to push his own agenda. President Donald Trump accused Bezos of using the newspaper to push for his own personal interests and to help Amazon.

The Washington Post

sold during the holidays. A year later, more than nine million were sold worldwide during the holiday season alone, making 2016 the company's best holiday shopping season to date.

As sales of the Echo and the Dot, its smaller companion smart speaker, were surging, so was Amazon's workforce. Since its humble beginnings in Bezos's garage, the company had steadily outgrown each office space it occupied. In 2010, Amazon moved its corporate headquarters to a towering 1.6 million-square-foot

(148,645-sq-m) building in an industrial neighborhood north of Seattle's downtown district. That building, which occupied a full city block and featured a set of three glass spheres (akin to the pyramids fronting the entrance to the Louvre Museum in Paris, France), provided space for more than 10,000 employees. But even that wasn't enough room for Amazon's continued growth.

So, in 2017, Amazon started searching for a location for its second headquarters—known throughout the company simply as "HQ2." By the deadline for proposals, 238 cities across the United States and Canada had submitted bids full of incentives to entice Amazon to choose them, including tax cuts and prime real estate options. Becoming the site of an Amazon headquarters would bring up to 50,000 jobs and billions of dollars to whichever city was selected. Major metropolitan areas pulled out all the stops to woo the company. New York City lit up landmarks such as the Empire State Building and One World Trade Center in "Amazon Orange"; New York's governor offered to change his name to Andrew "Amazon" Cuomo if the company choose to settle in the Big Apple. "The case for New York City is simple: We are the global capital of commerce, culture, and innovation," New York mayor Bill de Blasio wrote in a letter to Bezos.

A year after starting its search, Amazon announced that it would split its second headquarters between two cities: Long Island City, New York, and Arlington, Virginia. Each city would be home to 25,000 employees and receive an investment of more than $2.5 billion from Amazon.

The Spheres outside Amazon
corporate headquarters in Seattle

Politics and Pandemics

Amazon started its 25th year in 2019 at the top of its game. It accounted for almost half of all online sales in the United States and employed more than 640,000 people worldwide. But that success came with growing pains, as was evidenced by the negative reaction to its HQ2 plans in New York City. Although many leaders had gone to great lengths to lure the company to the city, not everyone was thrilled about Amazon's arrival in the Big Apple.

OPPOSITE: Face masks were a highly sought-after item on Amazon during the COVID-19 pandemic of 2020.

Amazon's intense warehouse tracking methods and fast pace can lead to employee injuries and burnout.

On the day after Long Island City was announced as one of two locations for a new Amazon campus, residents started protesting. They were joined by local politicians who disagreed with the tax cuts and other benefits that had been offered to the company. Union officials and other advocates were critical of the way Amazon treated employees.

n the weeks that followed, opposition grew. Amazon tried holding rallies with supporters and sending fliers to residents. Nothing helped. On February 14, 2019, Amazon withdrew its HQ2 offer from New York,

AMAZON

citing a lack of support from local and state politicians. It would focus its new headquarters solely in Arlington, Virginia, as well as a smaller hub in Nashville, Tennessee.

But within a year, discussions of Amazon's physical locations would become far less prominent. When the COVID-19 pandemic started in early 2020, Amazon's online shopping model saved the day for customers who no longer had access to necessities in their local stores. It was the perfect alternative for those who weren't comfortable going to public places, where they could

During the pandemic, brick-and-mortar stores saw a big drop in customer traffic.

possibly contract the virus. More people started working from home, and schools established remote learning programs. Online shopping for everything from groceries and cleaning supplies to soundproof headphones and office supplies took off. So did Amazon's profits. Thanks

AMAZON

to a 37 percent growth of sales in the third quarter of 2020, the company recorded quarterly profits of $6.3 billion—an increase of 197 percent over the third quarter the previous year.

I t wasn't just retail sales that were thriving. The efforts Amazon had made to vary its offerings over the years paid off during the pandemic. Amazon Web Services, which had started in 2003 as a platform to host e-commerce sites for other businesses, grew tremendously as more businesses looked to move sales online. Prime Video, the company's

Richest Man in the World

In July 2018, Jeff Bezos's **net worth** grew to more than $150 billion, which earned him the title of "richest man in the world." He stayed on top for the next two years, eclipsing the $200 billion mark in 2020, thanks to Amazon's sales during the pandemic. By 2023, Bezos had handed the crown to Tesla founder Elon Musk and slipped to third place among richest people. But by then, Bezos had decided to donate most of his money to causes he cares about—primarily fighting climate change and bridging social and political divisions.

In 2020, Amazon employee numbers jumped more than 60 percent worldwide over 2019.

streaming service, saw a dramatic increase in the number of subscriptions. More families stayed home to binge-watch shows and movies during pandemic-related lockdowns and quarantines.

To keep up with demand, Amazon announced that it would be hiring up to 100,000 more employees, many of them warehouse workers. Those opportunities were a boon to retail workers and others who had been laid off. But they also put thousands of people near each other in crowded warehouse settings. Concerns about safety conditions led to a walkout by employees at a Staten Island warehouse in March 2020. Employees at locations in Michigan and Illinois soon did the same. Workers across the company took to social media to voice their complaints, which led to discussions about organizing to protect themselves. "We need to unionize nationwide to have a voice for health and better working conditions," an employee from Texas posted on a Facebook group for Amazon workers.

Amazon fiercely opposed the unionization efforts. Unions give employees negotiating power that can force a company to increase salaries and benefits and upgrade safety protocols, which can have a negative impact on profitability. Amazon invested millions of dollars campaigning against union votes at several locations across the country. By the end of 2022,

Calls to unionize at Amazon have been part of the company's history since the beginning.

Jeff Bezos (*second from left*) and crew of Blue Origin's first manned flight, 2021

only one location, a warehouse in Staten Island, had successfully voted to unionize.

midst the pandemic and employee unrest, Jeff Bezos stepped down as Amazon CEO on July 5, 2021—exactly 27 years after launching the company. Although he would stay on as executive chairman, he was letting go of day-to-day operations. He wanted to focus on philanthropic projects, climate change, and space exploration—including a trip to outer space in a rocket built by his company, Blue

Pre-Prime

Before there was Amazon Prime, there was Super Saver Shipping. It allowed Amazon shoppers to pay a lower rate for shipping because their orders waited until there was room on the trucks, which sometimes delayed delivery. The reduced delivery cost led some shoppers to add more products to their online carts. Amazon believed that Prime's subscription-based free delivery would lead to even more sales. They were right. Prime created "Amazon Addicts" who shopped for books, clothing, and food on the site. "It was really about changing people's mentality so they wouldn't shop anywhere else," said Vijay Ravindran, the director of ordering services when Prime was introduced in 2005.

Origin. "I've never had more energy, and this isn't about retiring," Bezos wrote in a letter to employees announcing the change early in 2021. "I'm super passionate about the impact I think these organizations can have."

Bezos named Andy Jassy, who had worked for Amazon since 1997, as his successor. Jassy inherited a company that was experiencing record sales and huge profits. But it was also a company that had been embattled by lawsuits and unionization efforts and

"I've never had more energy, and this isn't about retiring. I'm super passionate about the impact I think these organizations can have."

was still figuring out how to manage operations during a pandemic. Although most of those factors were out of his control, Jassy's first year was marked by a 40 percent plunge in Amazon's stock price—the biggest decline since the dot-com bust in 2001.

Things got worse in 2022. Record inflation, rising interest rates, and major supply chain issues wreaked havoc on Amazon's earnings and led to one of the company's worst financial performances in its history. Jassy was forced to take a large pay cut himself, but he also had to eliminate thousands of jobs. By spring of 2023, more than 27,000 job cuts had been announced. Construction of the company's HQ2 facility in Arlington, Virginia, had been paused.

Amazon has been through similar ups and downs in its history and has proven that it can come through better than before. As it invests more in new ideas, from robots and drones to space-age satellite networks, it will continue to search for the next big thing that will propel it into the future—and allow it to continue providing everything customers need, delivered right to their doors.

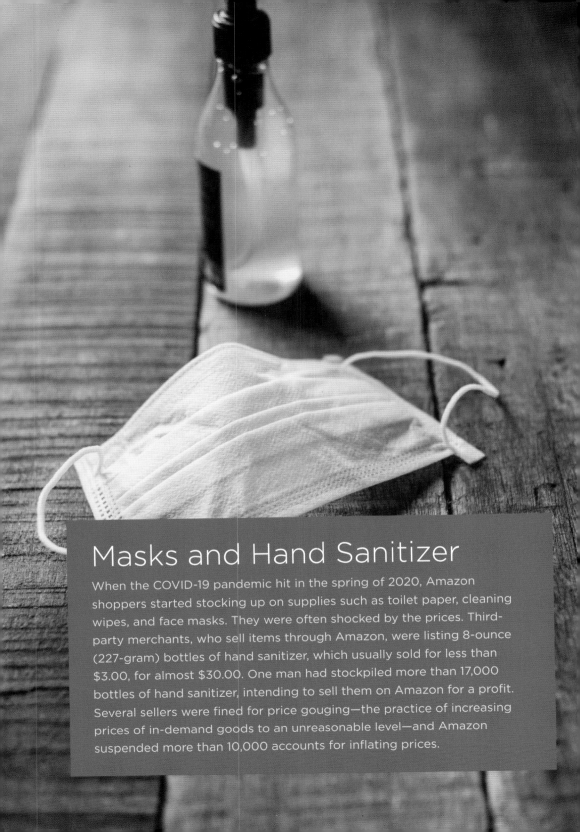

Masks and Hand Sanitizer

When the COVID-19 pandemic hit in the spring of 2020, Amazon shoppers started stocking up on supplies such as toilet paper, cleaning wipes, and face masks. They were often shocked by the prices. Third-party merchants, who sell items through Amazon, were listing 8-ounce (227-gram) bottles of hand sanitizer, which usually sold for less than $3.00, for almost $30.00. One man had stockpiled more than 17,000 bottles of hand sanitizer, intending to sell them on Amazon for a profit. Several sellers were fined for price gouging—the practice of increasing prices of in-demand goods to an unreasonable level—and Amazon suspended more than 10,000 accounts for inflating prices.

Selected Bibliography

"Amazon.com, Inc. history, profile, and history video." CompaniesHistory.com. Accessed May 20, 2023. https://www.companieshistory.com/amazon-com.

Bryar, Colin, and Bill Carr. *Working Backwards: Insights, Stories and Secrets from Inside Amazon*. New York: St. Martin's Press, 2021.

Dumaine, Brian. *Bezonomics: How Amazon Is Changing Our Lives and What the World's Best Companies Are Learning from It*. New York: Scribner, 2020.

Ramo, Joshua Cooper. "1999 Person of the Year: Jeffrey P. Bezos." *Time* magazine., December 27, 1999.

Stone, Brad. *Amazon Unbound: Jeff Bezos and the Invention of a Global Empire*. New York: Simon & Schuster, 2022.

---. *The Everything Store: Jeff Bezos and the Age of Amazon*. New York: Back Bay Books, 2013.